This book is dedicated to young boys who dare to dream, no matter the circumstance you can succeed.

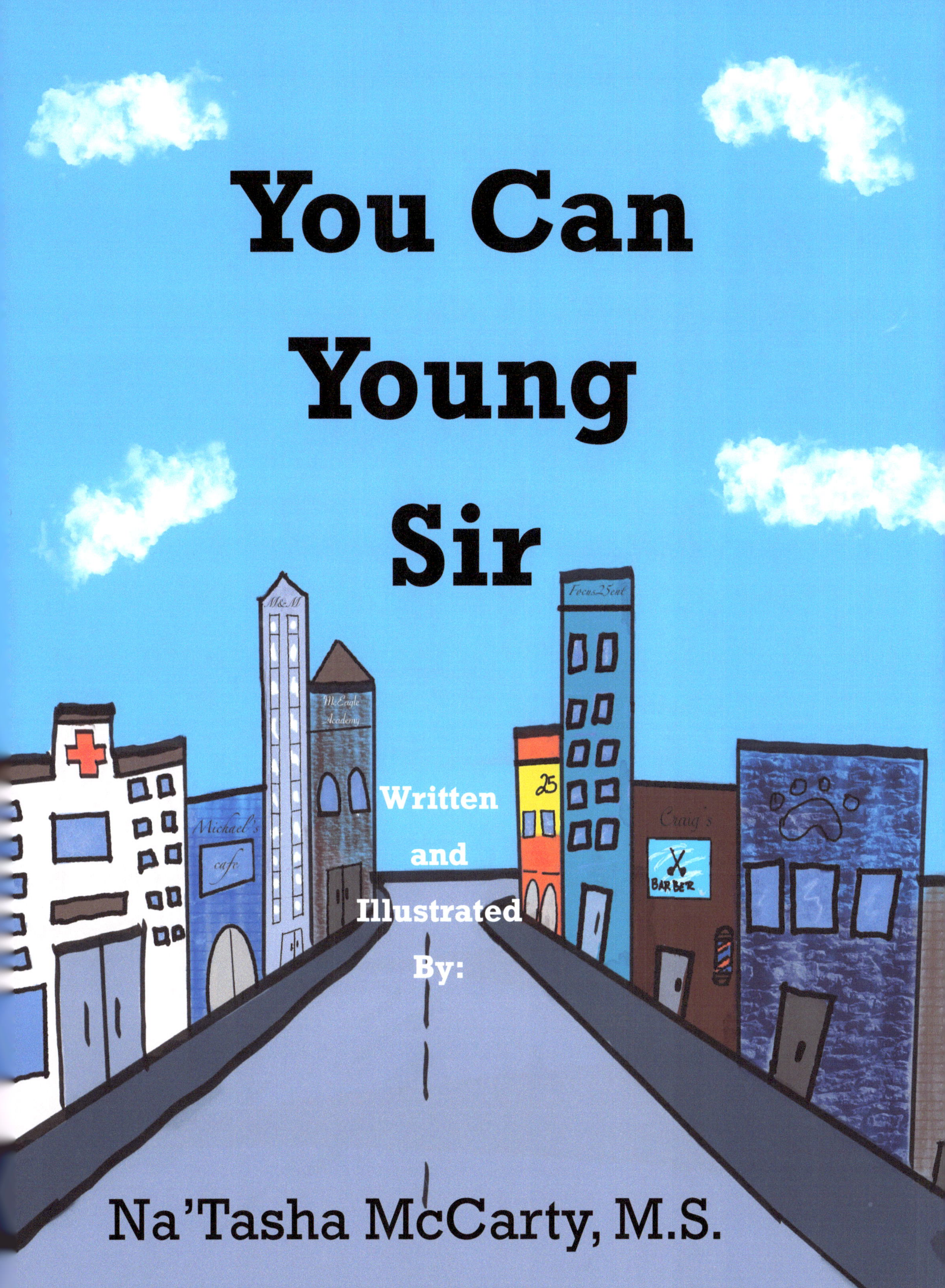

You Can
Young
Sir
Written
and
Illustrated
By:
Na'Tasha McCarty, M.S.

You Can Young Sir, what can you do you may ask, well anything you put your mind to and work hard for. Like what you may ask, well lets see the possibilities.

You can be a *Business Man or CEO* if you choose. These jobs run companies in order to make money and to help many people in the community. If you are a leader, creative, daring, and determined this may interest you. Well, if you put your mind to it and work hard, *you can.*

What about an *Architect or Engineer*? These jobs draw and design buildings and help fix roads. They help create new ways of doing things and help make changes to things to make them better such as machines or electronics. With determination and hard work, *you can*.

You Can Young Sir!

You may want to be a *Lawyer*. This job works in a court room to advise people on the law. If you like to defend people and speak in front of people this might be for you. Well, if you put your mind to it and work hard, *you can*.

What about a *Sports Agent*? This job finds talented players from all sports and helps them sign contracts to play for teams. It also assists athletes in managing their money and helps athletes get brand deals. If you like sports and can build relationships this may be for you. With determination and hard work, *you can*.

If you like telling stories then you might want to be an *Author*. This job uses imagination and writing skills to tell stories that convey messages for others to read about. Well, if you put your mind to it and work hard, *you can*.

What about becoming a *Teacher*? This job helps people explore and learn new things. With determination and hard work, *you can*.

You Can Young Sir!

You can be a *Doctor or a Nurse* if you chose. If you like science and helping people this could be for you. These jobs help keep people healthy and help people when they're sick. Well, if you put your mind to it and work hard, *you can*.

You can be a *Veterinarian* if you choose. This job helps animals feel better when they are sick or hurt. Well, if you put your mind to it and work hard, *you can.*

You Can Young Sir!

You can be a *Firefighter or a Police Officer* if you choose. These jobs help people stay safe as well as protect and serve the community. With determination and hard work, *you can*.

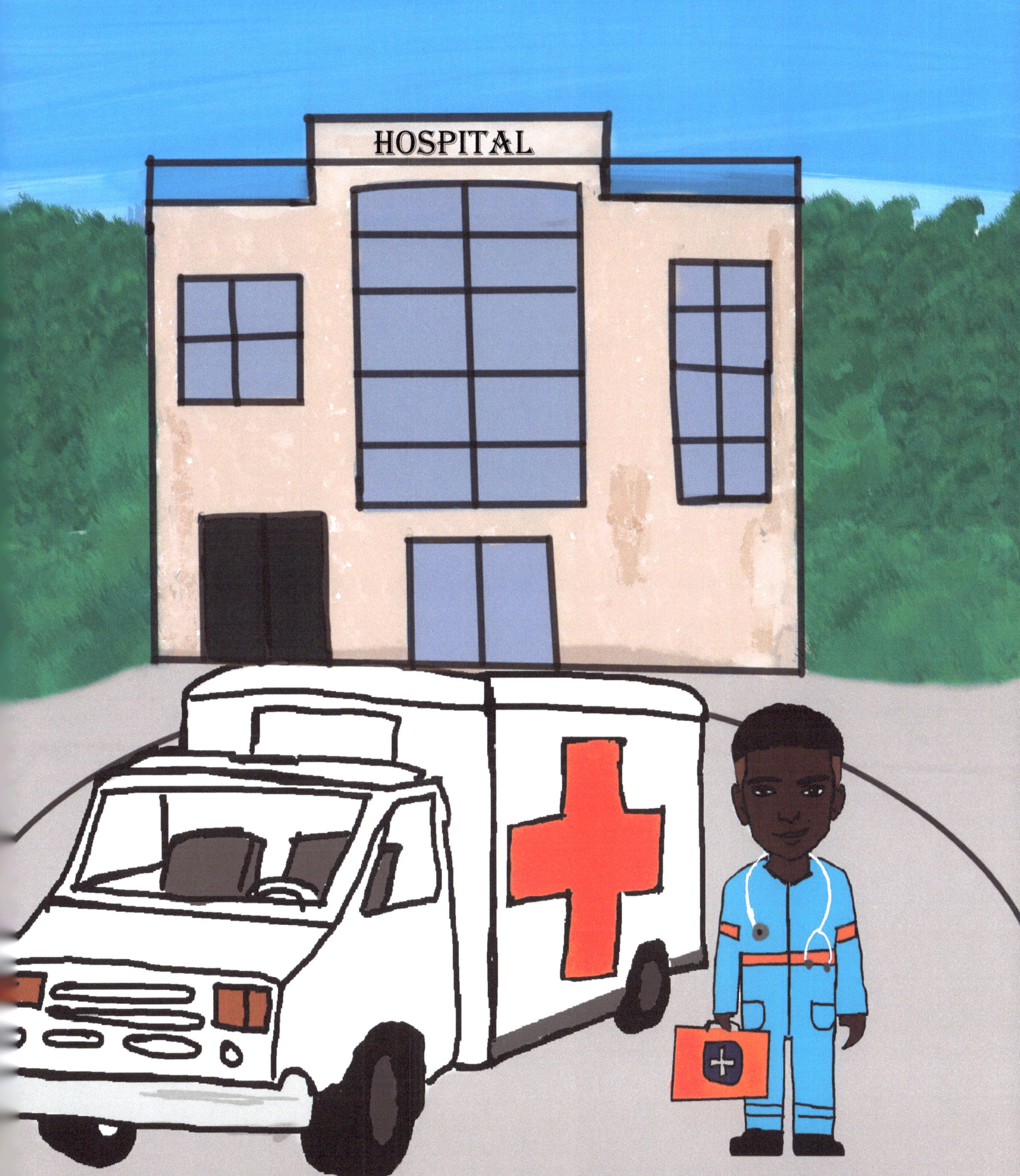

What about an *EMT or Paramedic*? These jobs help people when there is a health emergency. They help people feel better and serve the community. Well, if you put your mind to it and work hard, *you can*.

Perhaps you might want to be a *Truck Driver*. This job helps companies get products to people who need them. With determination and hard work, *you can*.

What about a *Barber*? This job helps people look and feel great by cutting and styling hair. With determination and hard work, *you can*.

You Can Young Sir!

If you like to talk and share your opinion, you might want to be a *Radio Personality or TV Broadcaster*. These jobs inform and entertain people. Well, if you put your mind to it and work hard, *you can*.

You can be a *Chef* if you choose. This job is where you cook incredible food items for people to enjoy. Well, if you put your mind to it and work hard, *you can*.

You Can Young Sir!

If you like computers or video games you might want to be a *Software or Computer Programmer*. These jobs create computer programs and video games using science and technology. Well, if you put your mind to it and work hard, *you can*.

Do you like to draw and create? If so, you can be a *Graphic Designer* if you choose. This job allows you to be creative as well as use technology. Well, if you put your mind to it and work hard, *you can*.

You Can Young Sir!

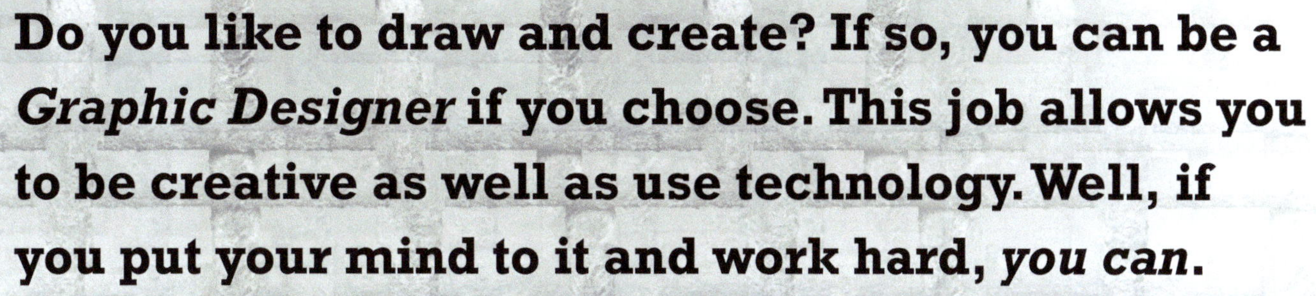

What about a *Realtor*? This job helps people find houses to live in or buildings for companies to work in. With determination and hard work, *you can*.

You can be a *Pilot* if you choose. This job flies planes to transport people or products to a desired destination. Well, if you like heights, seeing new places and adventure then this could be for you. With determination and hard work, *you can.*

You Can Young Sir!

So always remember if you work hard for what you want

You can young Sir!!

Architect
?????
Lawyer
Doctor
CEO
So Young Sir
what path will
you choose?

What are my interest?

What I want to be when I grow up

Goals

____

____

____

____

____

____

Steps to Attain My Goals

____

____

____

____

____

Goals

____

____

____

____

____

____

____

Steps to Attain My Goals

____

____

____

____

____

Goals

____

____

____

____

____

____

Steps to Attain My Goals

____

____

____

____

____

Goals

____

____

____

____

____

____

____

Steps to Attain My Goals

____

____

____

____

____

____

Acknowledgments

I would like to thank God with whom all things are possible. My mother (Dorothy) who has always loved, supported, and pushed me to always strive for greatness. My late father (Michael) who instilled in me at a young age to always work hard for my dreams and never give up. My brothers (Michael and Marcus) who have always been there for me and who has shown that hard work and dedication pays off. They have exemplified excellence and have challenged and defied stereotypes to achieve their goals. To my family and friends who have supported me through my journey.

Special thanks to Dorothy, Michael, Dominque, Craig, Marcus, Lindell, Jennifer, Joshua, Dyracka, Shaneak, Alicia